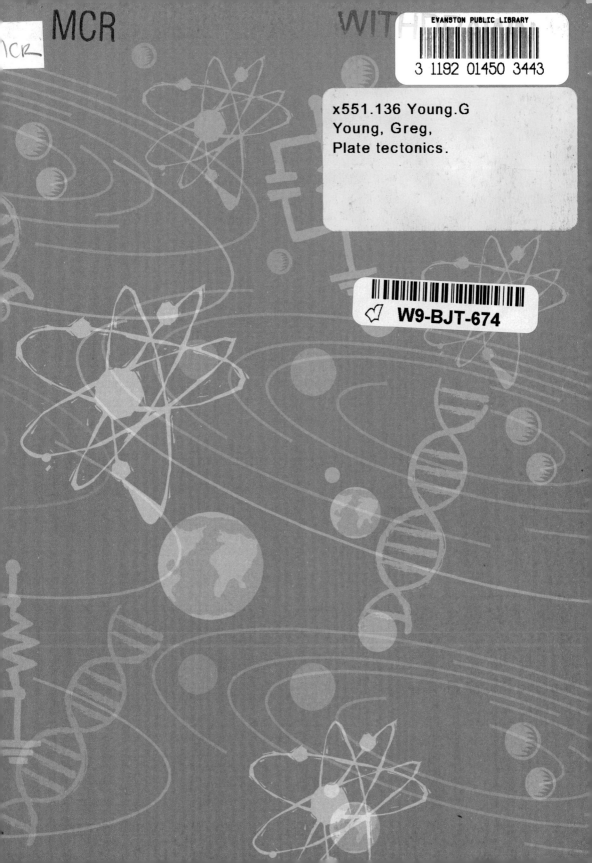

Plate Tectonics

by Greg Young

Science Contributor
Sally Ride Science
Science Consultants
Nancy McKeown, Planetary Geologist
William B. Rice, Engineering Geologist

MISSION: SCIENCE

Developed with contributions from Sally Ride Science™

Sally Ride Science™ is an innovative content company dedicated to fueling young people's interests in science.

Our publications and programs provide opportunities for students and teachers to explore the captivating world of science—from astrobiology to zoology.

We bring science to life and show young people that science is creative, collaborative, fascinating, and fun.

To learn more, visit www.SallyRideScience.com

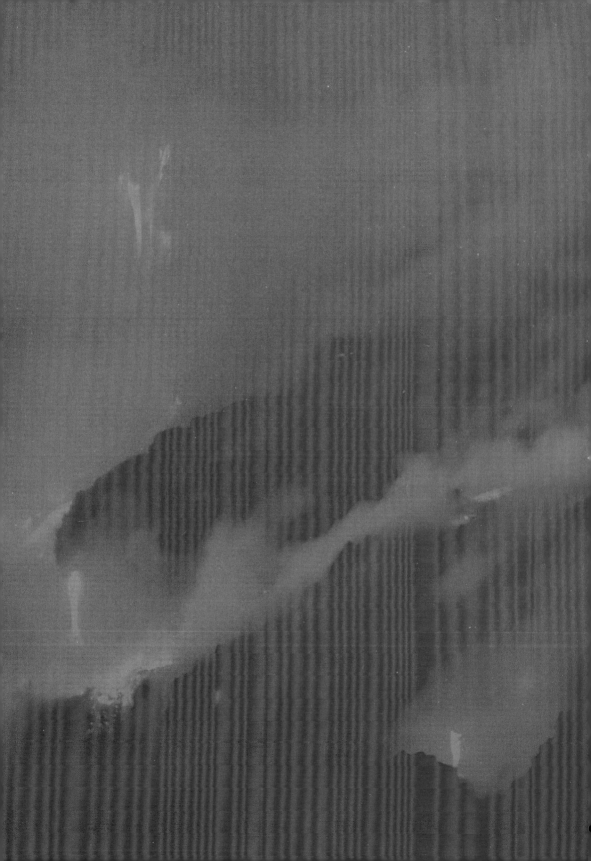

First hardcover edition published in 2009 by
Compass Point Books
151 Good Counsel Drive
P.O. Box 669
Mankato, MN 56002-0669

Editor: Jennifer VanVoorst
Designer: Bobbie Nuytten
Editorial Contributor: Sue Vander Hook

Art Director: LuAnn Ascheman-Adams
Creative Director: Joe Ewest
Editorial Director: Nick Healy
Managing Editor: Catherine Neitge

This book was manufactured with paper containing at least 10 percent post-consumer waste.

Library of Congress Cataloging-in-Publication Data
Young, Greg, 1968–
  Plate tectonics / by Greg Young.
   p. cm. — (Mission : science)
  Includes index.
  ISBN 978-0-7565-4232-0 (library binding)
  1. Plate tectonics—Juvenile literature. I. Title. II. Series.
  QE511.4.Y69 2009
  551.1'36—dc22   2009011450

Visit Compass Point Books on the Internet at *www.compasspointbooks.com*
or e-mail your request to *custserv@compasspointbooks.com*

Table of Contents

Earth's Shifting Crust

Imagine Earth as a huge egg. An egg has a shell, while Earth has a crust. An egg has liquid under its shell, while Earth has hot, runny magma beneath its crust. In the middle of an egg is a yolk. Earth also has a center: the inner core.

The distance from the shell of an average chicken egg to the center of its yolk is only about 1 inch (2.5 centimeters), but it would be a 4,000-mile (6,400-kilometer) trip from Earth's crust, through the mantle and outer core, to the center of the inner core.

Traveling inward, each layer grows hotter and hotter. Earth is hottest at the center of the core, where temperatures range from 7,200 to 9,000 degrees Fahrenheit (4,000 to 5,000 degrees Celsius). In fact, the core of Earth is hotter than the surface of the sun! The inner core is solid, pressed by the weight of the planet that surrounds it.

Sometimes liquid magma oozes through Earth's crust, reaching the planet's surface.

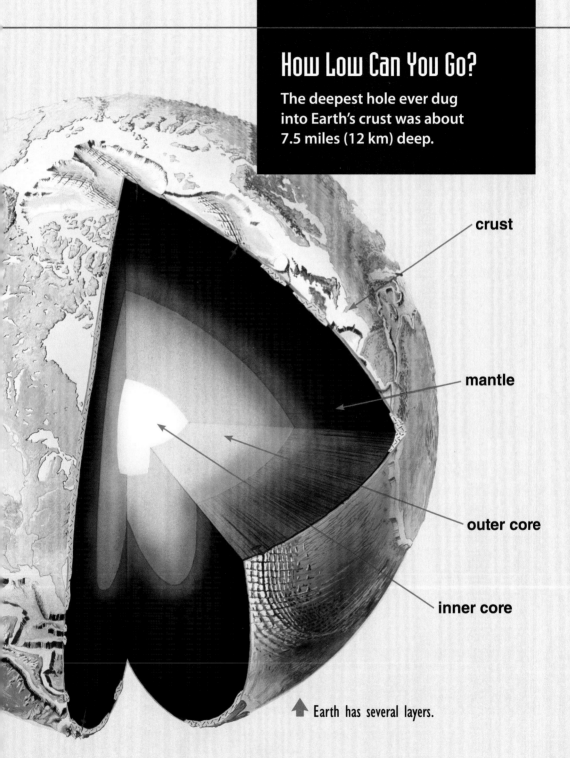

How Low Can You Go?

The deepest hole ever dug into Earth's crust was about 7.5 miles (12 km) deep.

crust

mantle

outer core

inner core

⬆ Earth has several layers.

We live on the lithosphere—the outer "shell" of Earth. This is the cool, rocky crust that makes up the continents, with their mountains, plains, and valleys. The ocean floor, with its sandy plains, chasms, and underwater mountain ranges, is also part of the lithosphere.

Carol Hirozawa Reiss

Marine geologist Carol Hirozawa Reiss works for the U.S. Geological Survey. Her job is to study the ocean floor. In 1994, aboard a submersible vehicle named *Turtle,* she plunged 1.4 miles (2,200 meters) to the dark floor of the North Pacific Ocean to investigate two tectonic plates that are spreading apart. Where the plates are parting, heat from beneath the crust escapes, and molten lava oozes up and forms an underwater mountain range called the Juan de Fuca Ridge. Reiss wrote down what she saw through the window of the submersible and worked with special equipment to measure how fast the tectonic plates on the seafloor were spreading apart. She also took careful notes about strange creatures such as tube worms that live where hot, acidic water gushes out of vents called black smokers.

Tube worms feed at the base ➡ of a black smoker vent.

Though Earth is like an egg in many ways, Earth's crust is not smooth like an eggshell. Instead it's more like an egg that has been cracked. Huge chunks of crust, called tectonic plates, support the planet's continents and oceans. Because the plates are not connected to one another, they are constantly moving and shifting. Some plates drift apart while others collide. Still others scrape as they slide past each other. In the process, they create landforms such as mountains and trenches and are responsible for phenomena such as volcanic eruptions, earthquakes, and tsunamis.

Tsunami!

On December 26, 2004, two tectonic plates in the Indian Ocean smashed together. One plate was forced underneath the other, setting off a powerful underwater earthquake. The quake pushed a huge amount of water outward in a circular pattern. It triggered a series of tsunamis that hit the shores of Indonesia, Malaysia, Thailand, India, Sri Lanka, and other Southeast Asian nations. Waves up to 100 feet (30.5 m) high killed 225,000 people in 11 countries.

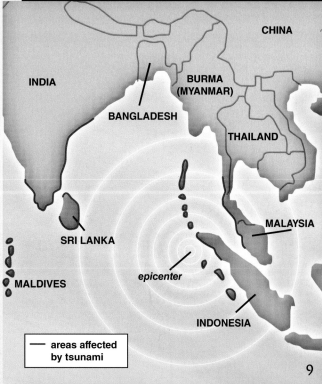

The epicenter of the 2004 earthquake was in the Indian Ocean, but the effects could be felt in many areas of Southeast Asia.

CHINA

INDIA

BURMA (MYANMAR)

BANGLADESH

THAILAND

SRI LANKA

MALAYSIA

MALDIVES

epicenter

INDONESIA

— areas affected by tsunami

9

Continental Drift

The ideas behind the theory of plate tectonics have been around for a long time. As early as the 1500s, some scientists believed that the continents had not always been in the same place. But it wasn't until 1912 that German meteorologist Alfred Wegener began writing and lecturing about the theory of continental drift, as he called it. Wegener believed that the continents used to be one large single landmass that he called Pangaea, a word that means "entire Earth." He said it was no coincidence that the

▲ Alfred Wegener

shapes of the continents appeared to fit together like puzzle pieces.

Wegener also pointed out that the coasts of Africa and South America that face each other across the Atlantic Ocean contained fossils of the same early animals and plants. He

◀ Wegener believed that Earth's continents had once formed a single landmass.

explained that the animals could not have swum across the ocean, and the plants were not adaptable to both climates. He concluded that the continents must have once been attached. Wegener also explained how the continents may have moved. He hypothesized that two forces caused the shift: the pull of the sun and moon and the daily spin of Earth.

Many geologists didn't accept Wegener's theory. They could see that some continents looked as if they might fit together, but most of them thought it was a coincidence. They also believed that the forces Wegener named were too weak to move the giant continents. Some of them had another explanation. They believed that land bridges had once connected the continents and were now sunk beneath the oceans. Although land bridges did exist, we know today that there weren't enough to explain all of the fossil similarities.

Wegener, who died in 1930, didn't live long enough to discover the reason for continental movement. During the 40 years after his death, scientists learned more about Earth's crust by mapping the seafloor. They bounced sound waves off the bottom of the ocean and recorded how long it took them to return. These sonar measurements confirmed earlier reports that an underwater mountain range circled the globe, much like the seams on a baseball.

The Mid-Atlantic Ridge is part of the underwater mountain range known as the mid-ocean ridge.

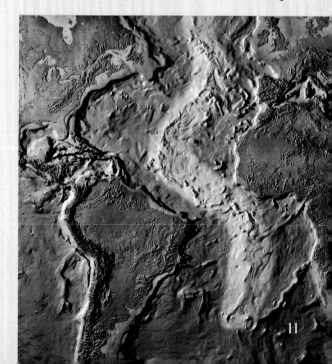

The Mid-Atlantic Ridge is part of this seafloor mountain range. It stretches about 6,200 miles (10,000 km) and splits nearly the entire Atlantic Ocean from north to south. Scientists discovered that the Mid-Atlantic Ridge has a deep trench down the center. The trench is a crack in Earth's crust, the space between tectonic plates. Hot, molten magma pushes up through the crack from the asthenosphere, the layer below the lithosphere. As the magma rises, it pushes the two plates apart.

Magma that reaches the surface of Earth is called lava. The lava that emerges from the crack seeps onto the ocean floor, where it cools and becomes new rock at the center of the ridge.

New rock is continually accumulating along either side of the crack, expanding the undersea mountain range. In some places, parts of the range can be seen towering above the surface of the water, forming islands such as Iceland, the Azores, and Bermuda.

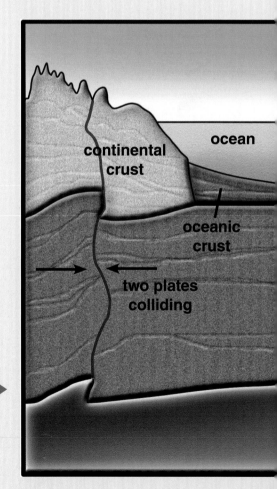

ocean

continental crust

oceanic crust

two plates colliding

Earth's plates move and interact in a variety of ways, each with a different effect on the planet.

The discovery and mapping of the Mid-Atlantic Ridge answered many questions geologists had about the movement of continents. It supported Wegener's theory of continental drift and led to an understanding of plate tectonics. And as more and more evidence was found to support the theory of plate tectonics, Wegener became more respected. Plate tectonics was eventually accepted by scientists. Today it is a basic part of geology.

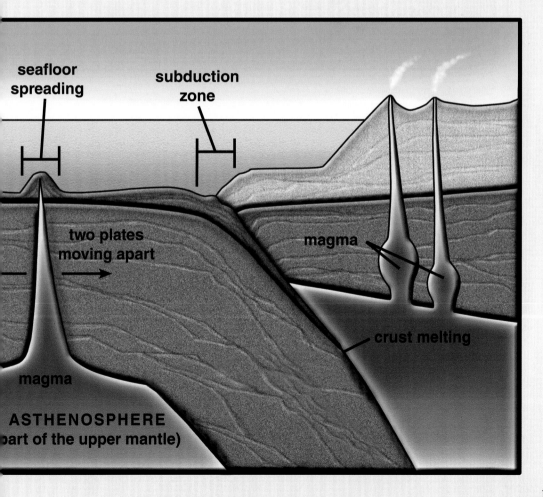

seafloor spreading

subduction zone

two plates moving apart

magma

crust melting

magma

ASTHENOSPHERE
(part of the upper mantle)

Unusual Stripes

After scientists mapped the Mid-Atlantic Ridge, they studied the volcanic rocks that formed the mountain range. They discovered that molten lava contains a natural magnetic mineral called magnetite that lines up in the direction of Earth's magnetic field. When the lava hardened, the magnetite "stood still," forming unusual stripes in the rock.

Scientists were puzzled that not all the magnetite pointed north. The mineral in the rocks farther away from the ridge pointed south. A little farther out,

the magnetite pointed north again. Then another strip pointed south. Scientists concluded that Earth's magnetic polarity must flip from time to time. The unusual striped rock was their clue to this so-called magnetic pole reversal.

More research revealed that the ridge widened about 1 inch (2.5 cm) every year. By observing how fast the ridge moved apart, geologists could determine how often the magnetic polarity flipped. They found that flips occurred about three or four times every million years.

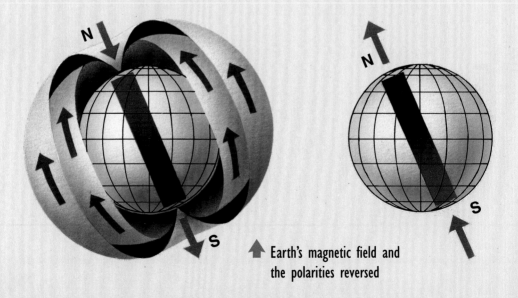

Earth's magnetic field and the polarities reversed

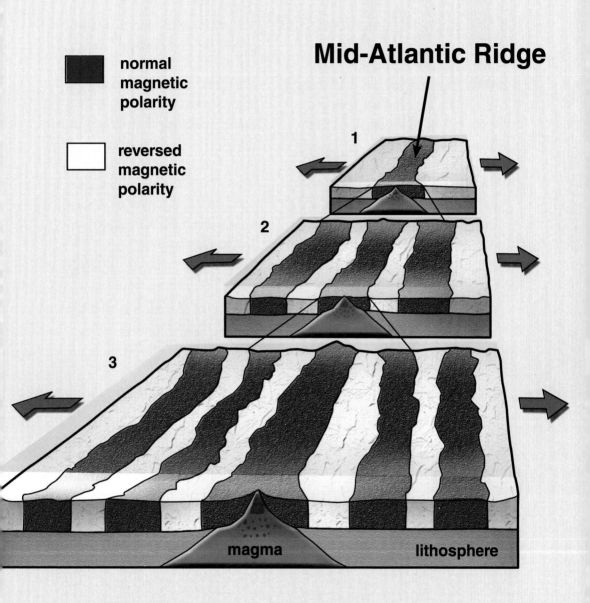

Mid-Atlantic Ridge

normal
magnetic
polarity

reversed
magnetic
polarity

1

2

3

magma lithosphere

The changes in Earth's magnetic field make a pattern on the
seafloor. Each time the field changes, a new stripe is made when
lava flows. Over time the changes create a striped pattern.

The crack between the plates in the Atlantic Ocean is continually widening. Molten magma rises to the surface through the crack, making new crust along the ocean floor. But does that mean that Earth's crust is getting bigger all the time? Geologists say no. They concluded that if Earth oozed molten magma in one place, then it must be swallowing up crust somewhere else. The rocks must be recycling.

Studies began to show that although the Atlantic Ocean floor is, indeed, expanding, the Pacific Ocean seafloor is shrinking. Scientists found that the plates under the Pacific seafloor are moving toward each other, colliding in slow motion.

Ring of Fire

ASIA

NORTH AMERICA

ASIA

EUROPE

AFRICA

SOUTH AMERICA

AUSTRALIA

Volcanoes form along areas where plates collide. The Ring of Fire is a circular area of plate boundaries with frequent volcanic activity.

Sometimes the edge of one plate gets pushed under the edge of a heavier plate. The sunken area is called a subduction zone. The edge of the sunken plate is forced down into the hot mantle, which melts the rock and recycles it back into magma.

The expanding and shrinking ocean floors are an example of how Earth recycles. Rocks are created from magma and are later recycled back to Earth's mantle.

Earthquakes and volcanoes result from tectonic activity. Most occur near undersea ridges and subduction zones. The plates that crash into each other cause Earth to tremble. Volcanoes erupt when the recycled rock returns to molten lava and erupts through an opening in the crust.

Newest Land on the Planet

When a volcano erupts, lava flows onto Earth's crust, where it cools and hardens to form new land. The island of Hawaii was formed and continues to expand from the lava flow of active volcanoes. One of them—Kilauea—frequently pours lava over a flat area of Hawaii. The lava burns everything in its path, forming new rock as it moves. It eventually steams to the ocean where it cools and forms more new rock.

Some volcanoes erupt deep below the surface of the ocean. These seamounts, as they are called, take thousands of years to get tall enough to reach the ocean's surface and form an island. Loihi, an erupting seamount near Hawaii, is taller than Mount St. Helens in Washington. Still, it is not expected to rise to the surface of the ocean for tens of thousands of years.

Kilauea is an active ➡ volcano on Hawaii, one of the Hawaiian Islands.

Plate Boundaries

Earth's crust is made up of 14 major tectonic plates and numerous minor ones. Major plates can be as wide as several thousand miles, while minor ones measure only a few hundred miles across. Plates that are even smaller are called microplates. Geologists have named the plates. Some are named after oceans, while others are named after continents, countries, or even the explorers who discovered them.

The edge along which tectonic plates meet is called a plate boundary. Plates have three main types of boundaries: divergent, convergent, and transform.

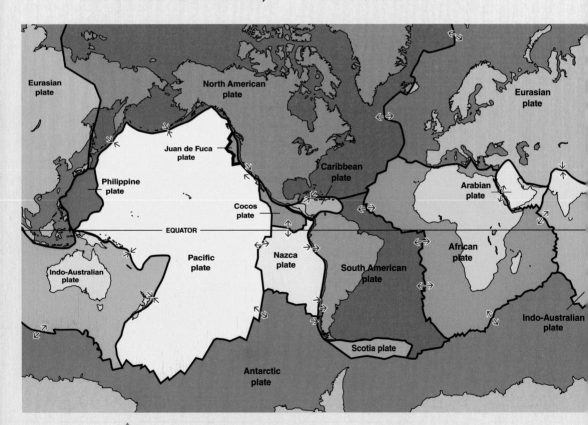

Earth's crust is made up of tectonic plates, which collide and pull apart, creating volcanoes, earthquakes, tsunamis, and other natural phenomena.

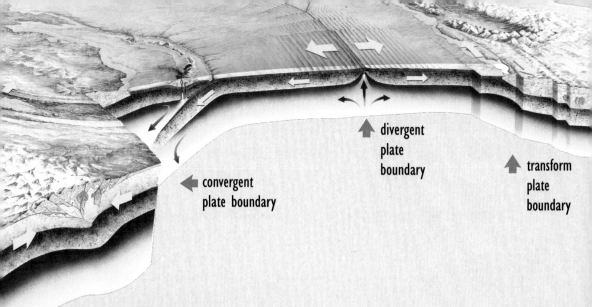

Divergent Boundaries

A divergent boundary occurs when two tectonic plates move away from each other. An example of a divergent boundary is where the North American and Eurasian plates are slowly spreading apart. The result is the Mid-Atlantic Ridge. Iceland, the small island in the northern Atlantic Ocean between Norway and Greenland, was formed at a divergent boundary when these two plates moved apart. The crack allowed hot, molten magma to rise and cool and then form new crust—an island—at the edges of the plates.

Volcanoes—nearly 200 of them—are a common sight in Iceland. The two plates that formed the island continue to move apart, allowing magma to burst up to the surface of the island and form volcanoes. Hot lava regularly flows out of the craggy center of the island where the two plates have left a crack in the crust. The island also has bubbling hot springs and geysers that regularly spew scalding water into the air.

The Great Rift Valley in eastern Africa is another example of a divergent boundary. The 2,100-mile (3,380-km) trench, formed by plates moving apart, stretches from Ethiopia to Mozambique.

Convergent Boundaries

A convergent boundary occurs when two plates move toward each other until they collide. When they crash, one of the plates has to give. Usually the lighter plate sinks, subducting underneath the heavier plate.

Scientists have classified convergent boundaries

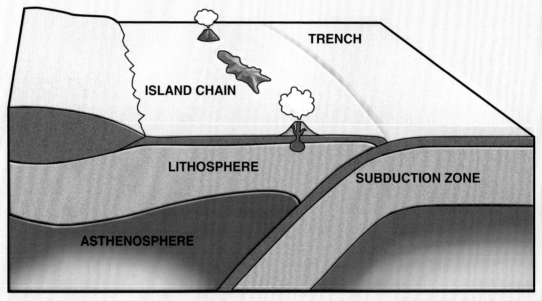

TRENCH

ISLAND CHAIN

LITHOSPHERE

SUBDUCTION ZONE

ASTHENOSPHERE

⬆ When plates collide at a convergent boundary, one plate sometimes subducts under the other.

Aleutian Islands

The Aleutian Islands off the coast of Alaska are the result of an underwater trench. The trench has created a wide volcanic mountain range that rises above the surface of the ocean. It forms the Aleutian Islands.

BERING SEA

Pribilof Islands

ALASKA

Unalaska   Dutch Harbor
Umnak   Fox Islands
Attu   Shemya Island

Kiska   Adak

Amchitka
Island

A L E U T I A N   I S L A N D S

according to the way they collide: an ocean-ocean collision, an ocean-continental collision, or a continent-continent collision.

An ocean-ocean collision occurs when two plate boundaries crash on the ocean floor. For example, in the Pacific Ocean, the fast-moving Pacific plate is crashing into the Philippine plate. At the point where they collide, the edge of the Pacific plate dives under the Philippine plate and melts into Earth's hot mantle. The result is the Mariana Trench in the northern Pacific Ocean. At a maximum depth of 6.8 miles (11 km), it is the deepest place on Earth.

Ocean-ocean collisions often result in earthquakes and volcanoes that spew molten magma from the asthenosphere. When these underwater volcanoes grow tall enough, they rise above the surface of the water. Just west of the Mariana Trench lies a stretch of 15 volcanic mountains that have poked their tops above the water and formed the Mariana Islands.

Deep and Creepy

Strange, creepy creatures live in the hot, murky depths of ocean trenches caused by tectonic activity. Fangtooth fish, sea pigs, and giant tube worms are just a few.

Fangtooth fish have rows of daggerlike teeth and milky-white spots where their eyes should be. Sea pigs slither along the ocean floor and munch on tasty morsels tucked into the mud. Giant tube worms flutter in moving, superheated water around belching vents on the sea floor. The water is heated by high temperatures beneath Earth's crust.

Volcano Chasers

Some scientists travel around the world studying volcanoes that are about to erupt. Their work often saves many lives because they can tell people how much time they have before an eruption. With enough warning, people can reach safety. To predict when a volcano will erupt, scientists measure the strength of earthquakes caused by magma rumbling beneath the surface of Earth. They also measure the amount of gases spewing from the volcano. A drop in gas pressure might mean the volcano is plugged, which could mean the eruption will be explosive and violent.

Did You Know?

The highest mountains on the planet might be getting even taller. Geologists suggest that the movement of the tectonic plates in the area is adding to the height of the Himalayas at the rate of about 0.16 inches (4 millimeters) per year.

An ocean-continental collision happens when an oceanic plate is subducted under a continental plate, a tectonic plate that supports land. An example is the shorelines of Peru and Chile in South America. There the Nazca plate is subducting under the South American plate. In the water, the subduction causes a deep trench to form. On land, the South American plate is pushed up, forming the tall peaks of the Andes Mountains. Earthquakes and volcanoes are very common in this area of the world.

When two continental plates hit, it is called a continent-continent collision. The two plates "fight it out" before one plate finally subducts under the other. Before it subducts, a lot of crust scrapes off of it, causing rock to build up and form hills and mountains. The Himalayas, a mountain range along the border between the Indian subcontinent and the Tibetan plateau, has the highest mountains in the world. They are the result of the Indian plate's being driven below the Eurasian plate.

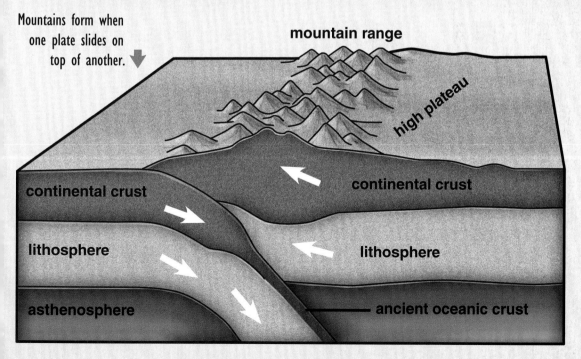

Mountains form when one plate slides on top of another.

mountain range

high plateau

continental crust

continental crust

lithosphere

lithosphere

asthenosphere

ancient oceanic crust

Transform Boundaries

A transform boundary occurs when tectonic plates slide past each other. The plates move in opposite horizontal directions and scrape their edges instead of smashing into one another.

Stretching north and south along western California lies the San Andreas Fault. Beneath California, the Pacific plate is slowly creeping northwestward. The North American plate is moving in the opposite direction. As the two plates scrape past each other, rocks along the boundaries sometimes get locked together and stop the plates from moving. When that happens, stress builds

up until finally one plate breaks loose from the other. The ground shakes and produces an earthquake.

One of the worst natural disasters in U.S. history was the earthquake that hit San Francisco on April 18, 1906. The quake occurred when one of the plates under the San Andreas Fault suddenly moved 20 feet (6 m) in just a few seconds. As a result,

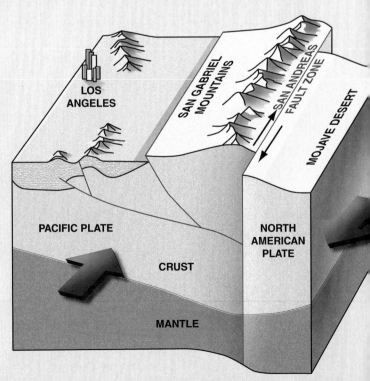

LOS ANGELES

SAN GABRIEL MOUNTAINS

SAN ANDREAS FAULT ZONE

MOJAVE DESERT

PACIFIC PLATE

NORTH AMERICAN PLATE

CRUST

MANTLE

a 296-mile (476-km) section of the fault shook for about 42 seconds. Tremors were felt hundreds of miles away. The San Francisco earthquake and the fire that followed claimed more than 3,000 lives.

Living on a Fault

The small town of Parkfield in west-central California is on a section of the San Andreas Fault where earthquakes occur regularly. The town lies at a point where a locked section of the fault to the south meets a creeping segment to the north. On September 28, 2004, one of the plates moved about 18 inches (46 cm), setting off a large earthquake and strong aftershocks that lasted more than a week.

San Andreas Fault
━━━━ Locked
━━━━ Creeping

North American plate

San Francisco

Parkfield

Pacific plate

Los Angeles

The San Andreas Fault is a transform boundary.

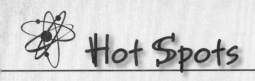

Hot Spots

Most earthquakes and volcanic eruptions happen where tectonic plates meet. But there are other areas—called hot spots—where molten magma has been seeping up or spewing out of the asthenosphere for years. These volcanoes occur in the middle of oceanic plates and continental plates.

Hot spots in the ocean have formed islands such as Hawaii. The large island currently sits on top of a hot spot. But Hawaii was not always over that hot spot, nor will it stay there. The Pacific plate that lies underneath is constantly moving northwestward. The hot spot, however, does not move. At one time, the hot spot formed the island of Kauai at the western end of the Hawaiian Islands chain.

The island of Hawaii has the only active volcanoes in the islands. But as the Pacific plate continues to move, the

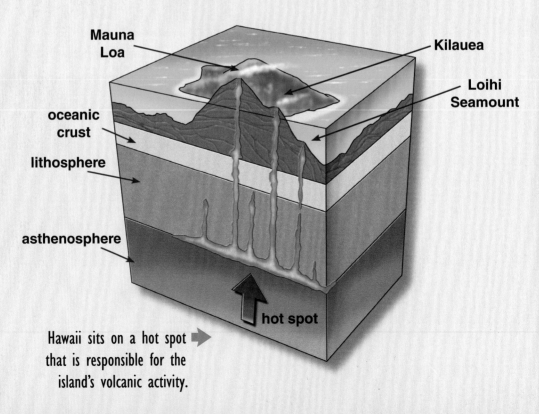

Hawaii sits on a hot spot that is responsible for the island's volcanic activity.

volcanoes will no longer be above the hot spot and so will cease to be active. Perhaps the hot spot will one day form a new island in the Pacific Ocean.

Each Hawaiian island was created by a hot spot's volcano before the plate moved.

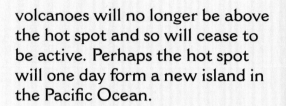

Kauai
Oahu
Molokai
Lanai
Maui
Hawaii

Volcano Viewing

At the Hawaii Volcanoes National Park, red-hot rivers of lava ooze out of the island's two active volcanoes. Cooled, hardened lava forms bumpy ribbons on new land that forms every day. Some of the lava flows down the hillside in fiery orange streaks, ending up in the ocean. When the hot lava meets the cool salt water, billows of steam drift into the air. Visitors to the park can observe Earth's drama from the safety of marked trails.

The thermal pools at Yellowstone National Park are always warm because of the hot spots deep below them.

On land hot spots produce hot springs, pools of bubbling mud, and geysers such as Old Faithful in Wyoming's Yellowstone National Park. The huge crater in which the park sits was formed after a huge volcanic eruption that occurred hundreds of thousands of years ago. The Snake River Plain, located mainly in Idaho, was formed from the hot spot that Yellowstone now sits above. The curved shape of the plain follows the northwestward path the North American plate followed as it moved over the hot spot.

Tectonic plates are always moving, which means Earth is constantly changing. Throughout time, Earth has been modified and its matter recycled. Continents have moved, and coastlines have been altered. Earth will continue to change in the future. Some changes will be slow, while others will be swift, brought on by sudden disasters that alter the land or the water. But plate tectonics will continue to help us understand Earth's past changes, and to predict how it will change in the future.

The Snake River in Wyoming is on a plain formed by a hot spot.

Evidence of volcanic activity is visible throughout Yellowstone.

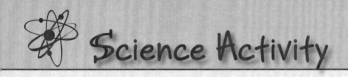

Getting to the Core

By digging deep into Earth's crust, geologists can get an idea of what our planet looks like inside. They can't dig all the way to the core, however, so they have to find other ways to learn about Earth's center. Geologists use earthquakes to help them "see" inside the planet.

An earthquake sends shock waves through Earth. Earthquake waves travel through solids and liquids differently. When geologists receive earthquake data, they can tell whether the waves have passed through solid or liquid material. By recording and analyzing data from many earthquakes, geologists have gained a fairly accurate idea of what Earth looks like inside. A core sample would provide more accurate information, but it is not yet possible to get one.

To get an idea of what it would be like to take a core sample of Earth, try this activity. You will drill core samples from an egg to see what it looks like inside.

Materials

- hard-boiled egg
- plastic drinking straw
- plastic knife
- scissors

Procedure

1   Crack and peel the shell off the hard-boiled egg.

2   Hold the egg in one hand and insert the straw into the top of the egg with your other hand. Slowly but firmly, press the straw through the center of the egg and out the other side.

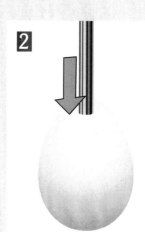

3   When the straw exits the other side of the egg, you will see parts of the egg in the straw. This is your core sample. As you continue to push, you will see a part of the straw that doesn't have any egg in it. Cut the straw at this point.

4   Pull the remaining part of the straw out of your egg. You can dig another core sample from a different location on your egg with the rest of the straw. Try entering the egg from a different angle.

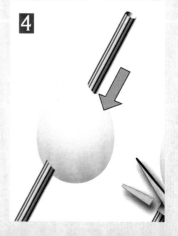

5   Again, when the straw exits the egg, cut it off when you no longer see any egg inside.

6   Use your scissors to cut open your straw pieces. Be careful not to damage the samples with the scissors. Examine your core samples.

7   Based on your core samples, draw a picture of what you think your egg looks like on the inside.

8   After you have drawn your picture, slice the egg open with the plastic knife. How close was your drawing to the actual egg?

Conclusion

Geologists take core samples of Earth to learn what the planet looks like inside. The data they gather helps them understand the planet's innermost makeup and recognize changes over time.

Florence Bascom (1862–1945)
American geologist and one of the first female geologists;
studied mountains and how they are formed

Samuel Warren Carey (1911–2002)
Australian geologist who was an early advocate of the theory
of continental drift; developed the theory of the expanding
Earth, which proposes that Earth's volume is increasing, causing
the formation of tectonic plates

William Maurice Ewing (1906–1974)
American oceanographer who made detailed maps of the
sea bottom using refraction of waves caused by explosions
(similar to sonar); helped describe the Mid-Atlantic Ridge,
an area of spreading seafloor in the Atlantic Ocean

Beno Gutenberg (1889–1960)
German-American geologist who determined the boundary
between Earth's mantle and core, based on the behavior of
earthquake waves

Harry Hammond Hess (1906–1969)
American geologist who developed the theory of seafloor
spreading, in which new crust develops at mid-ocean ridges
and is destroyed at deep sea trenches

Charles Francis Richter (1900–1985)
American seismologist who developed a scale for measuring
the intensity of earthquakes, called the Richter scale

Marie Tharp (1920–2006)
American geologist who, with research partner Bruce Heezen,
discovered a valley in the middle of the Mid-Atlantic Ridge and
published a map of the entire ocean floor

Alfred Wegener (1880–1930)
German geologist and meteorologist who suggested the idea
of continental drift—that the continents once fit together into
a supercontinent he named Pangaea

1620	English scientist Francis Bacon notices the jigsaw fit of opposite shores of the Atlantic Ocean
1760	English geologist John Michell suggests that earthquakes are caused by one layer of rocks rubbing against another
1828	First measurement of Earth's magnetic field
1906	Earthquake waves are first used to identify Earth's layers
1907	American scientist Bertram Boltwood uses uranium to determine the age of rocks
1912	German meteorologist Alfred Wegener proposes the theory of continental drift
1915	Wegener writes *The Origin of Continents and Oceans,* in which he argues for his theory of continental drift
1925	German expedition uses sonar to confirm the existence of the Mid-Atlantic Ridge, a mountainlike ridge through the Atlantic and Arctic oceans resulting from the separation of tectonic plates
1935	American seismologist Charles Francis Richter develops a scale to determine earthquake intensity
1950s	Scientists, including American geologist Harry Hammond Hess, discover odd magnetic variations across the ocean floor
1958	Australian geologist Samuel Warren Carey publishes *The Tectonic Approach to Continental Drift,* an essay in support of the expanding Earth theory

1960	Hess proposes seafloor spreading, lending credibility to Alfred Wegener's theory of continental drift
1968	French geophysicist Xavier Le Pichon publishes a complete model of Earth based on six major tectonic plates and their motions
1969	Core sample data from deep sea research vessel *Glomar Challenger* provides conclusive evidence for seafloor spreading and, as a result, continental drift
1977	American oceanographers John Corliss and Robert Ballard discover deep-sea vents around the Galapagos Islands in the Pacific Ocean; American geologists Marie Tharp and Bruce Heezen publish a map showing the geologic features of the entire ocean floor
1985	American oceanographer Peter Rona finds the first deep-sea vents in the Atlantic Ocean
1990	Oldest portion of the Pacific plate is found
2007	American geologist Vicki Hansen proposes that early meteorites created the first cracks in Earth's crust, which she says jump-started the movement of Earth's tectonic plates
2009	German scientists create a mathematical model for calculating the future position of continents

Glossary

asthenosphere—layer of soft, hot rock below the lithosphere

continent—single large area of land

continent-continent collision—collision of two continental plates, usually producing a mountain range between them

continental drift—theory that continents move from one place to another by the motion of gigantic plates that make up Earth's crust

continental plate—tectonic plate that supports one or more continents

convergent boundary—boundary where tectonic plates come together

divergent boundary—boundary where tectonic plates move apart

earthquake—sudden movement of Earth's crust caused by volcanic activity or the release of stress along plate boundaries

fault—break in the rock of Earth's crust

geologist—scientist who studies how Earth formed and how it changes by examining soil, rocks, rivers, and other landforms

geysers—springs that shoot hot water or steam into the air

hot spot—region of very hot magma in the mantle

lava—magma that comes out of a volcano

lithosphere—Earth's crust and the upper part of the mantle

magma—hot, molten rock beneath Earth's crust

magnetic—having the qualities of a magnet or capable of being attracted by a magnet

mantle—layer of hot rock between Earth's crust and core

Mid-Atlantic Ridge—area of seafloor in the Atlantic Ocean that is spreading apart because of divergent boundaries

ocean-continental collision—collision of tectonic plates in which an oceanic plate slides beneath a continental plate

oceanic plate—tectonic plate that is under the ocean

Pangaea—single landmass made of all of today's continents; means "entire Earth"

plate—gigantic slab of Earth's crust that moves around on magma

plate boundaries—edges of plates, which sometimes scrape or collide with each other

plate tectonics—theory that Earth's crust is made up of large slabs of rock that move about on molten magma

seamounts—underwater mountains rising from the ocean floor but still below the surface of the water

sonar—device that measures the distance to an object by bouncing sound waves off the object and timing how long it takes the waves to return

subduction—sinking of one plate edge beneath another

subduction zone—area where one plate is sinking beneath another plate, usually forming a trench

submersible—vehicle capable of operating or remaining underwater

tectonic plates—gigantic slabs of Earth's crust that move around on magma

transform boundary—boundary where tectonic plates slide past each other

tsunami—gigantic ocean wave created by an undersea earthquake, landslide, or volcanic eruption

volcano—vent in Earth's crust from which lava pours; mountain formed from the buildup of lava

Edwards, John. *Plate Tectonics and Continental Drift.*
North Mankato, Minn.: Smart Apple Media, 2006.

Fradin, Dennis, and Judy Fradin. *Witness to Disaster:
Earthquakes.* Washington, D.C.: National Geographic
Children's Books, 2008.

Harrison, David L. *Mountains: The Tops of the World.*
Honesdale, Pa.: Boyds Mills Press, 2005.

Rubin, Ken. *Volcanoes & Earthquakes.* New York:
Simon & Schuster Children's Publishing, 2007.

Stille, Darlene. *Plate Tectonics: Earth's Moving Crust.*
Minneapolis: Compass Point Books, 2007.

Internet Sites

FactHound offers a safe, fun way to find Internet sites related to this book. All of the sites on FactHound have been researched by our staff.

Here's all you do:
  Visit *www.facthound.com*
FactHound will fetch the best sites for you!

Greg Young

Greg Young has been a high school chemistry and physics teacher for 18 years. He enjoys sharing his interest in Earth science with his students. By demonstrating how the periodic table relates to mineralogy and the star life cycle and how Newtonian physics relates to satellites and moon phases, he provides students practical examples of the concepts they are learning. Practical examples are the "hook" in teaching science at any grade level.

Image Credits